观澜

Lan's Lens

一位摄影记者眼中的改革开放

王文澜 著
Wang Wenlan

China's Reform & Opening Up in the Eyes of a Photojournalist

中国画报出版社·北京
China Pictorial Press · Beijing

图书在版编目（CIP）数据

观澜：一位摄影记者眼中的改革开放：汉英对照 / 王文澜著 . -- 北京：中国画报出版社，2018.10
 ISBN 978-7-5146-1697-2

Ⅰ . ①观… Ⅱ . ①王… Ⅲ . ①改革开放 - 成就 - 中国 - 摄影集 Ⅳ . ① D619-64

中国版本图书馆 CIP 数据核字 (2018) 第 242956 号

Lan's Lens—China's Reform & Opening Up in the Eyes of a Photojournalist
Wang Wenlan
观澜：一位摄影记者眼中的改革开放
王文澜　著

出 版 人：于九涛
项目统筹：方允仲
责任编辑：刘晓雪
英文编辑：朱露茜
英文翻译：刘海乐
英文改稿：苏　格
英文审定：张　楠
图片编辑：刘　慧
美术设计：詹方圆
责任印制：焦　洋
出版发行：中国画报出版社
　　　　　（中国北京市海淀区车公庄西路 33 号 邮编：100048）
开　　本：16 开（787mm×1092mm）
印　　张：19.75
字　　数：150 千字
版　　次：2018 年 10 月第 1 版　2018 年 10 月第 1 次印刷
印　　刷：北京汇瑞嘉合文化发展有限公司
书　　号：ISBN 978-7-5146-1697-2
定　　价：168.00 元

总编室兼传真：010-88417359　版权部：010-88417359
发行部：010-68469781　010-68414683（传真）

《观澜：一位摄影记者眼中的改革开放》
编委会

主　任：
陆彩荣

副主任：
黄　卫

编　委：
陆彩荣、黄　卫、于九涛、赵　岭、方允仲

Lan's Lens
— China's Reform and Opening Up in the Eyes of a Photojournalist
Editorial Board

Director:
Lu Cairong

Vice Director:
Huang Wei

Members:
Lu Cairong　Huang Wei　Yu Jiutao　Zhao Ling　Fang Yunzhong

 照片的日子

我从出生之日,就和相机结下了不解之缘:从满月到周岁,从上学到工作,从结婚到生子,生活的轮回与生命的延续,都在镜头前真实生动地呈现着。从拿起相机开始,我又用镜头去拍摄人:人的心态、人的精神、人的处境、人的一切;变的与不变的,内在的和外部的,看得见的与看不见的。有了活生生的人,有了酸甜苦辣的味道,有了柴米油盐酱醋茶,照片就有了灵魂。

四十年一瞬间,中国像一个沸腾的大工地,在这个传统的国度里,正在进行着世界经济史上最伟大的实验。我们用高速发展取得了发达国家百年发展的文明成果,这样难得的历史机遇,正是摄影人大显身手之时。

摄影器材的日新月异给拍摄带来随心所欲的惊喜,这让摄影变得太容易,然而摄影难就难在太容易了。容易掌握的东西,也容易最终失去它,只有把镜头对准身边瞬息即逝的日子,即保存了珍贵的记忆,才能留住人类的历史。

在中国有上亿人的拍摄群体,每天都在产生着无数的照片。拍照如此有魅力,在拍别人之前,你就已经成为别人照片里的角色,所以每个人都是摄影师,都是在照片里长大的,照片可以唤醒我们沉睡的记忆,留下令人难忘的日子。

从胶片年代迈入数码时代,我们按下快门,得到的是触摸不到的一个个数据,唯一不变的是拿在手中的照片,瞬间凝固了千变万化的时空。一张照片是一句话,两张照片就是一个对话:对照变化、对照生活、对照情感、对照历史、对照世纪间。长年累月的相对性瞬间,就是一个人的影像史记。

当我举起相机时,就开始用照片说话,就像作家用笔,画家用颜料,作

曲家用音符，舞蹈家用形体一样。不同的是，摄影作为瞬间语言，是区别其他艺术的重要特性，也是摄影价值的最终体现。

好照片是来之不易的，用照片说话，说得明白，说得幽默，说得有分量，就要下功夫了。拍不出好片子，是摄影者经常面临的处境，这恰恰是产生好照片的土壤。关键在于取景框后面的头脑，这比手中的相机更重要，因为我们不是手握机器的机器。

好照片是千载难逢的，有价值的景象每分每秒都在消失，到了下个世纪回头看，人们可以写、可以画、可以演，唯独摄影过期作废，一不留神，我们只能留下空白。一张照片放在那里，像一幅画、一首诗、一支歌；或是一个故事、一段历史；也可以说什么都不是，只是一张照片。

好照片是不言自明的，摄影是门技术，也是一种精神。所有的智慧都在"咔嚓"之中了。瞬间千变万化，在一生拍摄中，好照片只是凤毛麟角。照片好坏之间只差一点，早点晚点都会与好照片无缘。我的照片几乎每张都差一点，我这辈子就是为了这一点点。

生活之广，历史之厚，一个瞬间只是一个碎片，我力求给变化的历程留下一些痕迹。摄影早已不是一种仪式，我比任何时候都渴望按动快门，日子的节奏有如呼吸一样，呼是抒发，吸是充实，偶然之中包含着积蓄的必然，按下快门就是释放，我想说的也都在这些照片里了。

Preface

Days in Photos

Since the day when I was born, my life has been connected to the camera. Through the lens of a camera, every unforgettable moment in my life—celebrations for the completion of my first month and my 100th day in the world, my first day at school, my first day of work, my falling in love, my wedding, and birth of my child—was vividly recorded as a witness to the reincarnation and continuity of life. From the moment I got my own camera, I focused the lens on people to shoot their mind, their inner world, their dilemmas, and everything else about them—whether it is inside or outside, visible or invisible. The photos have souls only when they demonstrate true feelings and document real lives.

Time flies. Over the past decades, China has been like a busy construction site. The greatest experiment ever in the history of the world economy is ongoing in this country known for ancient civilization. It has realized rapid development and made achievements that cost developed countries a century to accomplish. This provides historic opportunities for photographers to give full use to their talent to record this great era with their photographic works.

The increasing advancement in photography equipment makes photography an easy job: It seems that everyone can snap a beautiful picture anytime. However, such convenience also makes photography harder than before. The easier one thing can be got, the faster one may lose it. Only when a photographer pays attention to transient moments in daily life can he or she capture precious memories and document the history of humanity.

At present, some 100 million people in China are engaged in photography. They create numerous photos every day. Photography has a magic power. As you focus your camera on others, you become the subject of pictures shot by someone else. So, everyone can be a photographer and the one to be photographed. Every photo can awaken our unforgettable memories of the past.

As photography has moved from film to digital, we now press the shutter and get an array of untouchable data rather than a slide of negative film. One thing remains consistent: The printed photos freeze the moments in our lives. A picture is a monologue, and two pictures together compose a dialogue on the comparisons of changes in life, emotion, era and history. Through the photos I took to document historical moments over decades, I compiled a photographical history of the nation's reform and opening up from my personal perspective.

As I raise my camera, I speak with photos just like writers using their pens, painters using their pigments, composers using music scores, and dancers using their body language. The only difference is that photographers document transient moments in daily life. This is not only an important feature that distinguishes photography from other genres of art, but also an embodiment of the ultimate value of photography.

It isn't an easy task to create a good picture. It takes painstaking efforts to snap a picture that speaks clearly, humorously and meaningfully. Many photographers find it difficult to shoot a satisfying picture. Don't get discouraged because failure is the mother of success. The head behind the viewfinder is much more important than the camera in hands. Photographers aren't machines but the minds taking control of the camera.

Capturing a perfect picture happens once in a blue moon since valuable images elapse in just a minute or even a second. As we look back next century, we'll still reproduce today through writing, painting or performances. But photography is an art requiring instant response. Once a moment is gone, it is gone forever. A printed picture is like a painting, a poem or a song, and at the same time, it is the carrier of a story or an episode of history. In some people's eyes, however, it may be nothing but a photo.

A good picture speaks itself. Photography is not only a technique, but also represents a kind of spirit. All wisdom of a photographer bursts out at the moment he or she presses the shutter. However, one can only snap very few good pictures in a lifetime. There is a fine line between a good picture and a bad one. You'll miss a good picture whether you press the shutter sooner or later. Almost every photo I have shot is so close to perfect; I have committed my whole life to pursuing for such perfection.

Life is all-encompassing, and history is profound. Any moment recorded in photos is a transient fragment of life or history. I try to leave some traces of the changing process of life and history with my photos. Photography has long been no more ceremonial. I'm more eager to press the shutter than any moment in the past. The rhythms of life are like exhaling and inhaling; exhaling is a way of expression, and inhaling is a way of enrichment. Behind any success that seems accidental is necessary accumulation of experiences. Pressing the shutter is a way of releasing. All I want to say is in these photos.

Wang Wen Lan

观澜

Lan's Lens
— China's Reform & Opening Up
in the Eyes of a Photojournalist

一位摄影记者眼中的改革开放

1980.4

时尚潮品太阳镜
Fashionable women wearing sunglasses

北京八大处
Badachu Park, Beijing

2005.6

意大利威尼斯
Venice, Italy

假面舞会国人秀
Chinese people at a masquerade ball

1984.1

满堂腊梅报新春
Blooming wintersweet heralding the arrival of spring

上海城隍庙
Chenghuangmiao Market, Shanghai

2007.12

北京北新桥

Beixinqiao, Beijing

小丑送花美到家

A flower delivery boy dressed like a clown

1983.6

衬衫成了抢手货
A crowd of customers purchasing shirts

北京展览馆
Beijing Exhibition Center, Beijing

1985.3

重庆解放碑
Jiefangbei, Chongqing

应急全靠铁栅栏
An iron fence separating hasty shoppers from salesclerks

1982.1

买布做衣老习惯
Buying cloth to make garments

北京百货大楼
Beijing Department Store, Beijing

2016.5

北京门头沟
Mentougou District, Beijing

欧尚派对布拉吉
Models in traditional European dresses

1981.1

私人定制合身服
A crowd of buyers outside a custom-made garment store

北京东城
Dongcheng District, Beijing

2013.7

北京新世界百货商场
New World Department Store, Beijing

百里挑一如意装
Shoppers picking clothes

1985.12

立等可取真方便
A sewing stall

云南红河
Honghe, Yunnan

2004.10

浙江宁波
Ningbo, Zhejiang

批量制衣流水线
A garment workshop

如今闺女真敢穿
Young ladies in fashionable dresses

1998.8

北京龙潭湖
Longtanhu Park, Beijing

2003.8

山东青岛
Qingdao, Shandong

看谁穿得最凉快
Women in fashionable dresses

为民服务缝纫忙
Busy in sewing

1982.3

福建泉州
Quanzhou, Fujian

2009.8

云南巍山
Weishan, Yunnan

扎织片片彩云间
Making tie-dye fabric

环境卫生自身净
A cleaner resting outside a photo studio

1992.4

海南海口
Haikou, Hainan

2018.9

上海浦东
Pudong, Shanghai

从早到晚保清洁
A cleaner working at night

1987.10

时装盖住书香门

A clothes stall in front of a bookstore

北京西四

Xisi, Beijing

1994.5

辽宁鞍山
Anshan, Liaoning

什么好卖卖什么
A bookstore selling a variety of commodities

1983.3

日常生活的旗帜
Drying clothes on the street

江西景德镇
Jingdezhen, Jiangxi

2004.9

浙江宁波
Ningbo, Zhejiang

阳光灿烂的日子
Drying clothes on a sunny day

1988.4

头顶鲜花一辈子
An old woman wearing flowers on the head

广西柳州
Liuzhou, Guangxi

2013.2

天津蓟县 老娘从头花到脚

Jixian, Tianjin An old woman in colorful costume

1994.10

艺高不怕巷子深

A beauty salon hidden in the lane

北京大方胡同

Dafang Hutong, Beijing

2003.8

上海浦东
Pudong, Shanghai

美不胜收小天地
A boutique beauty salon

1997·7

以假当真苦练功
Practicing haircutting

海南海口
Haikou, Hainan

2004.3

广东江门

Jiangmen, Guangdong

头头是道花样多

Practicing haircutting in a beauty salon

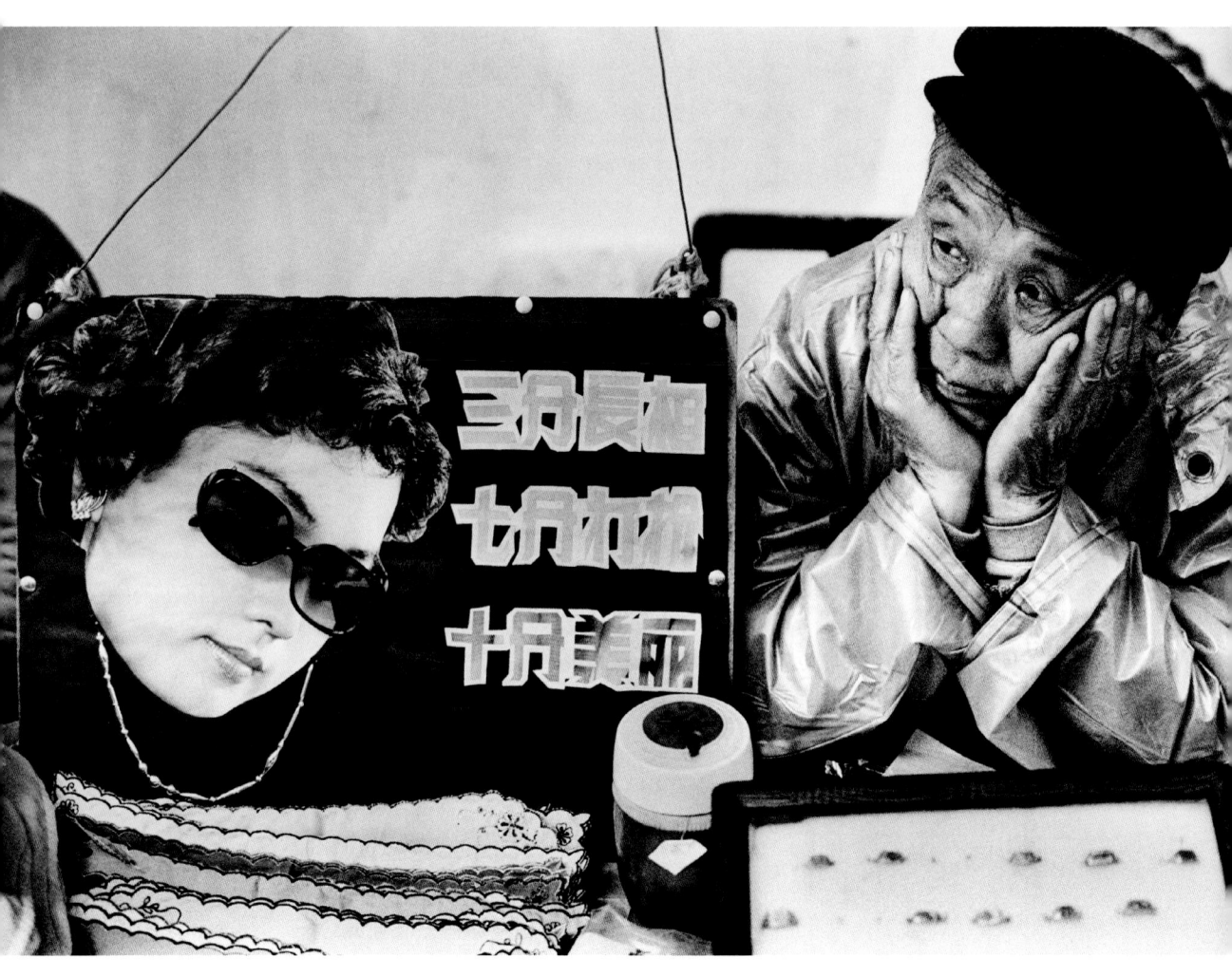

三分七分十分美
A jewelry stall on the street

1982.3

上海城隍庙
Chenghuangmiao Market, Shanghai

2008.1

北京秀水街
Silk Market, Beijing

珠光宝气梦中来
A jewelry stall

1983.9

模特设计齐亮相
A group photo of fashion models

北京民族文化宫
Cultural Palace of Nationalities, Beijing

2014.4

江苏南京 名牌广告争奇艳
Nanjing, Jiangsu   A huge advertising poster on the facade of a shopping mall

1986.11

金水桥上走猫步
Catwalk on the Golden Water Bridge

北京天安门
Tian'anmen, Beijing

1997·5

北京前门

Qianmen, Beijing

古都春色流行潮

Fashion springs up in ancient capital

1992.9

大牌箱包堆高塔

A mini Eiffel laid with LV suitcases

北京天坛公园

Temple of Heaven, Beijing

2012.5

北京农业展览馆
National Agricultural Exhibition Center, Beijing

金屋藏娇爱马仕
Hermes bags on display

1996.10

康熙雍正轮流坐
Enthroned as an "emperor"

北京故宫
Palace Museum, Beijing

2018.3

北京东城

Dongcheng District, Beijing

当今顾客是皇帝

The customer is "king"

2000.10

"清宫秘史"又一出　　　　　　　　　　　　　　　　　　　　　　　　北京故宫
Outside the Forbidden City　　　　　　　　　　　　　　　　Palace Museum, Beijing

2004.10

北京故宫 紫禁城前洋格格
Palace Museum, Beijing A foreign girl in Qing-style costume outside the Forbidden City

瞬间定格全家福
Taking a family photo

1984.1

河北玉田
Yutian, Hebei

1991.4

西藏拉萨
Lhasa, Tibet

我爱北京天安门
"I love Tian'anmen in Beijing"

1990.5

古为今用欠思量　　　　　　　　　　　　　　　　　　　　　　　　河南嵩山
Connecting to ancient statues　　　　　　　　　　　　　　　　Mt. Songshan, Henan

2004.9

山西平遥
Pingyao, Shanxi

宰相肚里能撑船
Probing the abdomen of the "chancellor"

正月社火齐下凡
A traditional opera troupe performing at the Spring Festival

1992.2

陕西陇县
Longxian, Shaanxi

2018.4

陕西府谷
Fugu, Shaanxi

花旦武生同下乡
Traditional opera artists going to the countryside

1988.2

骷髅之舞魔法师
Magic performance

北京地坛
Temple of Earth, Beijing

2018.9

上海正大广场
Super Brand Mall, Shanghai

骨感招牌吸眼球
Scaring decoration

1985.8

未雨绸缪雨中情
Watching games in the rain

北京工人体育场
Workers' Stadium, Beijing

2006.8

北京王府井
Wangfujing, Beijing

婚事喜逢世界杯
Wedding during the World Cup

1981.3

从小我是一个兵

Aspiring to become a soldier when growing up

北京工人体育场

Workers' Stadium, Beijing

1992.10

北京朝阳

Chaoyang District, Beijing

开学先当"花木兰"

Schoolgirls in military training

2005.9

越小越挑大的练
Playing with a toy gun

北京海淀
Haidian District, Beijing

2014.1

广西钦州
Qinzhou, Guangxi

我们都是神枪手
Little "snipers"

2004.9

鞋底赶超吉尼斯
A shoe sole listed in the Guinness World Record

山西平遥
Pingyao, Shanxi

2006.8

贵州都匀
Duyun, Guizhou

多大的码这都有
A huge cloth shoe

2006.5

上下遥望跨千年
A glance into the past

山东聊城
Liaocheng, Shandong

2011.5

甘肃华亭
Huating, Gansu

时空穿越握乾坤
Same smartphone, different costumes

百听不厌录山歌
Recording songs in a public performance

1988.4

广西柳州
Liuzhou, Guangxi

2017.7

湖南长沙

Changsha, Hunan

主播摄像一肩挑

Live broadcasting with smartphone

1993.3

京城迎来"思想者"
"Thinker" in Beijing

北京中国美术馆
National Art Museum of China, Beijing

2006.6

北京 798 艺术区
798 Art District, Beijing

抡出天地一片红
Red sculpture and red car

Lan's Lens
— China's Reform & Opening Up
in the Eyes of a Photojournalist

观澜

一位摄影记者眼中的改革开放

1978.12

全套把式奔地头
Going to work in the field

河北定县
Dingxian, Hebei

2013.11

湖南凤凰

Fenghuang, Hunan

牛前人后犁地忙

Plowing the field with a cattle-driven plough

1985.10

稻田收割一家人
A family harvesting rice

贵州锦屏
Jinping, Guizhou

2005.8

广西桂林 稻田里外靠一人

Guilin, Guangxi A farmer working in the paddy field

1982.3

购物还得挨个来
A long queue of people waiting to buy grain

上海老城
Old District of Shanghai

2008.10

北京山姆会员店
Sam's Club, Beijing

各种米面随意选
Bags of flour and rice packed in a supermarket

1983.10

翻山越岭赶大集
Crossing mountains to go to market

湖北西陵峡
Xiling Gorge, Hubei

2007.4

北京 798 艺术区
798 Art District, Beijing

行为艺术秀宠物
A performance artist and his pet

1989.12

随时品尝肯德基
A newly opened KFC restaurant in Beijing

北京宣武
Xuanwu District, Beijing

2017.8

北京前门　　　　　　　　　　　　　　　　　　　　山德士的中国梦
Qianmen, Beijing　　　　　　　　　　　　　　　Inside a KFC restaurant in Beijing

开业火爆麦当劳

Customers waiting in a long line outside in a newly opened McDonald's

1992.4

北京王府井

Wangfujing, Beijing

2018.8

北京王府井

Wangfujing, Beijing

汉堡"粉丝"金拱门

McDonald's is popular among youngsters in Beijing

1981.8

油条油饼豆腐脑

A food stall attracting numerous customers

北京朝阳

Chaoyang District, Beijing

2014.11

河北正定
Zhengding, Hebei

米粥馄饨小笼包
A street food stall selling steamed buns

1992.9

吃碗面条真便宜

A roadside noodles stall

北京西城

Xicheng District, Beijing

2015.7

北京前门

Qianmen, Beijing

这的卤煮挺正宗

A restaurant specializing in *luzhu* (pork lungs and intestines stewed with fried tofu and steamed bread)

京味楼里洋皇帝
A foreigner dressing like an emperor at a Beijing-style restaurant

2010.1

北京前门
Qianmen, Beijing

2018.9

上海浦东

Pudong, Shanghai

十里洋场土家宴

A Tu-style restaurant in Shanghai

庙会烧烤生意火

A popular barbecue stall

1985.2

北京地坛

Temple of Earth, Beijing

2016.1

北京王府井
Wangfujing, Beijing

王府串烧夜来香
A food stall offering hot and spicy sticks

1992.2

正月球场变饭场　　　　　　　　　　　　　　　　　　陕西陇县
Dining at a playground　　　　　　　　　　　　　　 Longxian, Shaanxi

2016.5

北京门头沟
Mentougou District, Beijing

盛夏球场变排档
Food stalls at a basketball playground

1998.4

有个地方就开张

An open-air food stall at the corner of the street

北京平安大道

Ping'an Avenue, Beijing

2015.9

上海静安 画中家园我们建
Jing'an District, Shanghai Food stalls on the street

2007.II

风餐露宿筑鸟巢
Constructors of the Bird's Nest

北京国家体育场
National Stadium, Beijing

2007.12

北京中央电视台新址
New Site of CCTV, Beijing

央视新楼平地起
New CCTV Building under construction

1981.4

玉泉山水真解渴
A roadside stall offering free spring water

北京海淀
Haidian District, Beijing

2015.9

四川双流

Shuangliu District, Sichuan

茶友聚此品百年

Sipping a cup of tea

1986.11

"中国可乐"大碗茶

Drinking "Big Bowl Tea," nicknamed "coke of China"

北京前门

Qianmen, Beijing

2016.3

北京前门

Qianmen, Beijing

传统茶馆新门帘

A traditional teahouse with a new door curtain

盛夏消暑凉西瓜
Escaping summer heat by eating watermelons

1981.7

北京三里屯
Sanlitun, Beijing

2005.10

北京海淀
Haidian District, Beijing

口味繁多冰激凌
Ice cream in varied flavors

1995.8

自产自销自逍遥
A farmer selling the watermelons he grew

北京西城
Xicheng District, Beijing

2017.7

北京前门
Qianmen, Beijing

现买现榨现品尝
A juice stall

1986.6

头顶烈日打生啤
Lining up to buy draught beer despite the scorching sun

北京西城
Xicheng District, Beijing

2011.8

北京蟹岛
Xiedao, Beijing

动感狂欢啤酒节
A beer drinking competition at the Xiedao Beer Festival

1983.10

众人抢收冬储菜　　　　　　　　　　北京四季青
Locals purchasing vegetables for winter　　Sijiqing, Beijing

2017.8

湖南长沙
Changsha, Hunan

一年四季品种多
A vegetable stall offering a variety of options

1985.11

京城处处大白菜
Beijing residents purchasing Chinese cabbages for winter

北京东城
Dongcheng District, Beijing

2016.4

北京农展馆
National Agricultural Exhibition Center, Beijing

造型艺术金白菜
Gold Chinese cabbage

1985.2

真够舔一阵子的

A kid eating candied haws on a long stick

北京地坛

Temple of Earth, Beijing

2018.3

北京鼓楼
Gulou, Beijing

冰糖葫芦串遍街
A sugar-coated haws stall on the street

2015.9

挑灯夜战垂钓园

Angling at night

北京门头沟

Mentougou District, Beijing

2017.12

吉林鸭绿江
Yalu River, Jilin

冰天雪地一网收
Catching fish from the iced river

1987.8

门庭若市供销旺
A bustling market

北京团结湖
Tuanjiehu, Beijing

2006.1

北京山姆会员店
Sam's Club, Beijing

满载而归迎新年
Purchasing goods for the Chinese New Year

1986.8

明码标价便宜卖
A roadside vegetable stall

四川成都
Chengdu, Sichuan

1995.10

北京南新华街

South Xinhua Street, Beijing

健康无价烟有价

A roadside cigarette stall

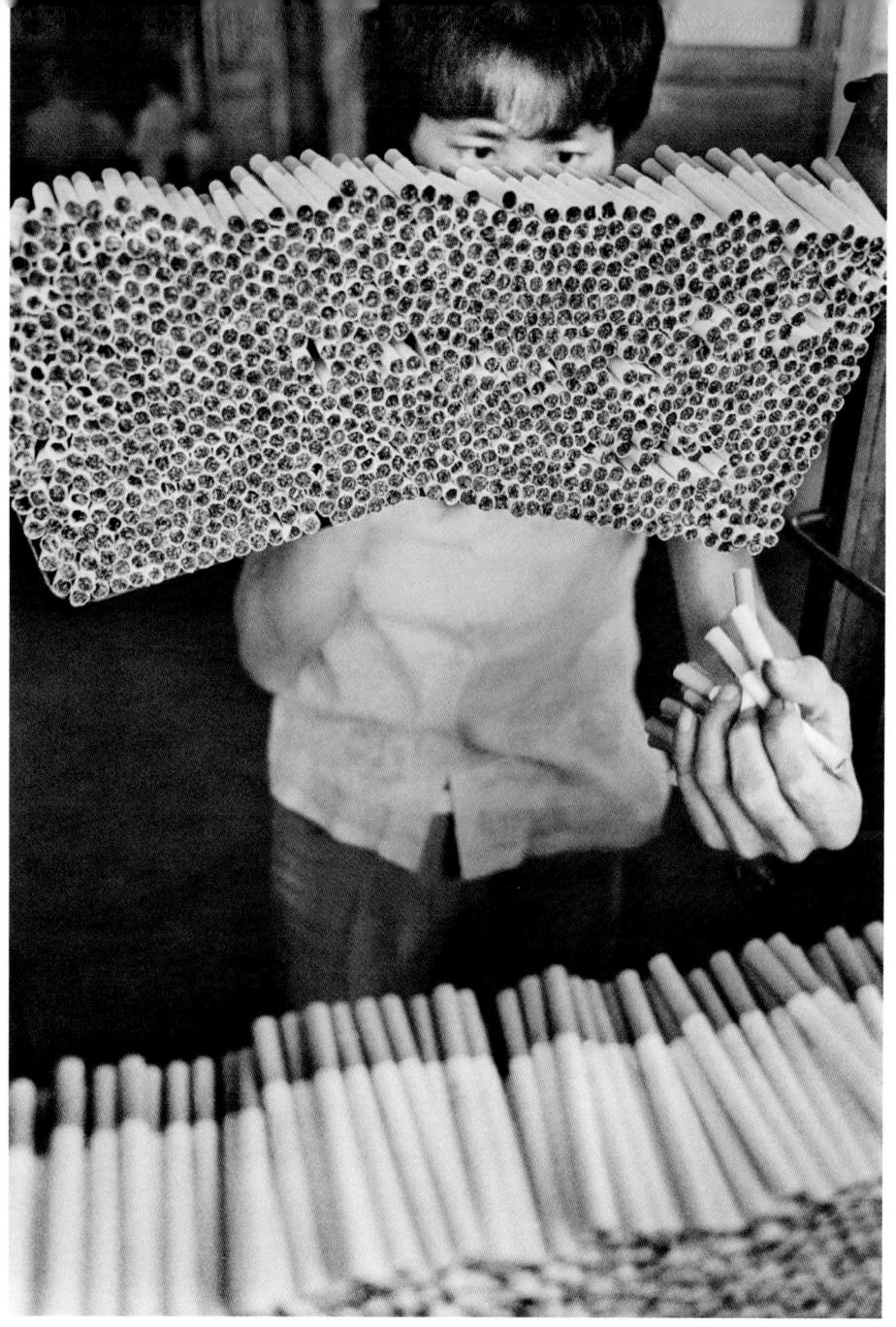

久抽肺部成蜂窝

Cigarettes arranged like a honeycomb

1988.4

广西玉林

Yulin, Guangxi

1988.4

北京天安门广场
Tian'anmen Square, Beijing

世界无烟日日讲
An activity promoting the World No-Smoking Day

1997·5

磨剪子嘞戗菜刀
A roaming scissors and knife polisher

北京海运仓
Haiyuncang, Beijing

2005.4

新疆喀什

Kashgar, Xinjiang

自行车的新用场

Polishing knife with a bicycle

外卖配送饿不着
A food delivery boy

2018.9

北京门头沟
Mentougou District, Beijing

2018.9

北京门头沟

Mentougou District, Beijing

足不出户品四方

Food delivery boys on the street

1992.6

个体书摊新风潮
A book stall in Beijing

北京北太平庄
Beitaipingzhuang, Beijing

2018.9

北京南锣鼓巷
Nanluoguxiang, Beijing

时尚汗衫正时兴
A boutique shop selling fashionable T-shirts

1996.4

晨报日报和晚报
A newspaper vendor

北京新街口
Xinjiekou, Beijing

2005.11

北京前门

Qianmen, Beijing

手机资讯随时看

Reading news on cell phone

1981.10

报中尽知天下事
Reading news on a bulletin board

北京劳动人民文化宫
Working People's Cultural Palace, Beijing

2015.6

北京三联书店

Sanlian Bookstore, Beijing

生活读书有新知

Reading books to learn knowledge

1987.6

小胡同里大书家

A calligrapher selling his works in a narrow lane

北京中剪子巷

Zhongjianzi Lane, Beijing

2004.11

北京前拐棒胡同
Qianguaibang Hutong, Beijing

代写书信渐消失
An old man providing transcription services, which is considered a dying profession

颜筋柳骨勤锤炼

Practicing calligraphy

1983.7

北京九道湾胡同

Jiudaowan Hutong, Beijing

2012.9

北京朝阳
Chaoyang District, Beijing

赤橙黄绿青蓝紫
Kids drawing in a kindergarten

1981.6

书山有路勤为径
Spending every available moment reading

北京北海公园
Beihai Park, Beijing

2007.3

北京北沙滩
Beishatan, Beijing

"五四"精神卷中寻
Searching the spirit of the May Fourth Movement in books

1988.8

大人小孩闲不住

A mother buying fruits while taking care of her kid

北京官园

Guanyuan, Beijing

2018.9

上海浦东
Pudong, Shanghai

我看平板你看书
A father reading a book and his kid watching an iPad

各得其乐小天地

A father enjoying a painting and his son playing on the ground

1985.4

北京中国美术馆

National Art Museum of China, Beijing

2005.5

北京翠微大厦

Cuiwei Plaza, Beijing

各取所需新追求

A father and his son in reading

2003.10

出家入门书中悟
Monks in a bookstore

北京大学
Peking University, Beijing

2017.12

北京王府井
Wangfujing, Beijing

学贯中西通古今
A customer in traditional costume and a foreigner in a bookstore contrasting each other

1981.5

满载图书把家还   北京王府井

Resting on the books they bought   Wangfujing, Beijing

2006.12

北京西单图书大厦 休闲度假好去处
Xidan Books Building, Beijing An ideal place to relax through reading

1994.5

音乐试听发烧友
A music fan

北京北新桥
Beixinqiao, Beijing

2005.3

北京新光天地
Shin Kong Place, Beijing

古典摇滚立体声
Music fans in a CD store

加减乘除靠算盘
Kids learning abacus calculation

1991.3

江苏兴化
Xinghua, Jiangsu

2014.12

北京三里屯　　　　　　　　　　　　　　　　　　　　　　男女老少买"苹果"

Sanlitun, Beijing　　　　　　　　　　　　　　　　　　　In an Apple store

1991.3

不用珠算心来算

Writing calculation answers on the blackboard

江苏兴化

Xinghua, Jiangsu

2005.5

北京农业展览馆
National Agricultural Exhibition Center, Beijing

互联网中天地宽
Surfing the internet

1993.6

街头传授算盘经
An abacus calculation class on the street

北京西单
Xidan, Beijing

2005.9

北京燕莎购物中心
Lufthansa Shopping Center, Beijing

网络上阵父子兵
A father and his son playing online games

观澜

Lan's Lens
—— China's Reform & Opening Up
in the Eyes of a Photojournalist

一位摄影记者眼中的改革开放

1983.2

双喜临门四合院
A wedding in a traditional quadrangle residence

北京丰盛胡同
Fengsheng Hutong, Beijing

2015.10

河北遵化
Zunhua, Hebei

新家新郎接新娘
A Benz limousine at a rural wedding

震耳欲聋天降喜
Thunderous firecrackers

1992.2

陕西凤翔
Fengxiang, Shaanxi

2015.10

河北遵化　　　　　　　　　　　　　　　　　　　　　礼炮齐鸣满地彩

Zunhua, Hebei　　　　　　　　　　　　　　Red remnants after explosion of saluting guns

1986.5

就想上班近一点
Exchanging for a house closer to workplace

北京劳动人民文化宫
Working People's Cultural Palace, Beijing

2007.12

河北石家庄 上下左右随意购
Shijiazhuang, Hebei Buying a better home

1986.5

房子能换不能买
Looking for a bigger house

北京劳动人民文化宫
Working People's Cultural Palace, Beijing

2003.6

北京东三环
East Third Ring Road, Beijing

新盘靠近国贸桥
Examining renderings of new buildings in CBD

1995·4

永远消失的风景
The scenery that lost forever

北京国英胡同
Guoying Hutong, Beijing

2013.1

北京鼓楼
Gulou, Beijing

旧城改造"拆"与"留"
Dismantling old houses in the central axis of Beijing

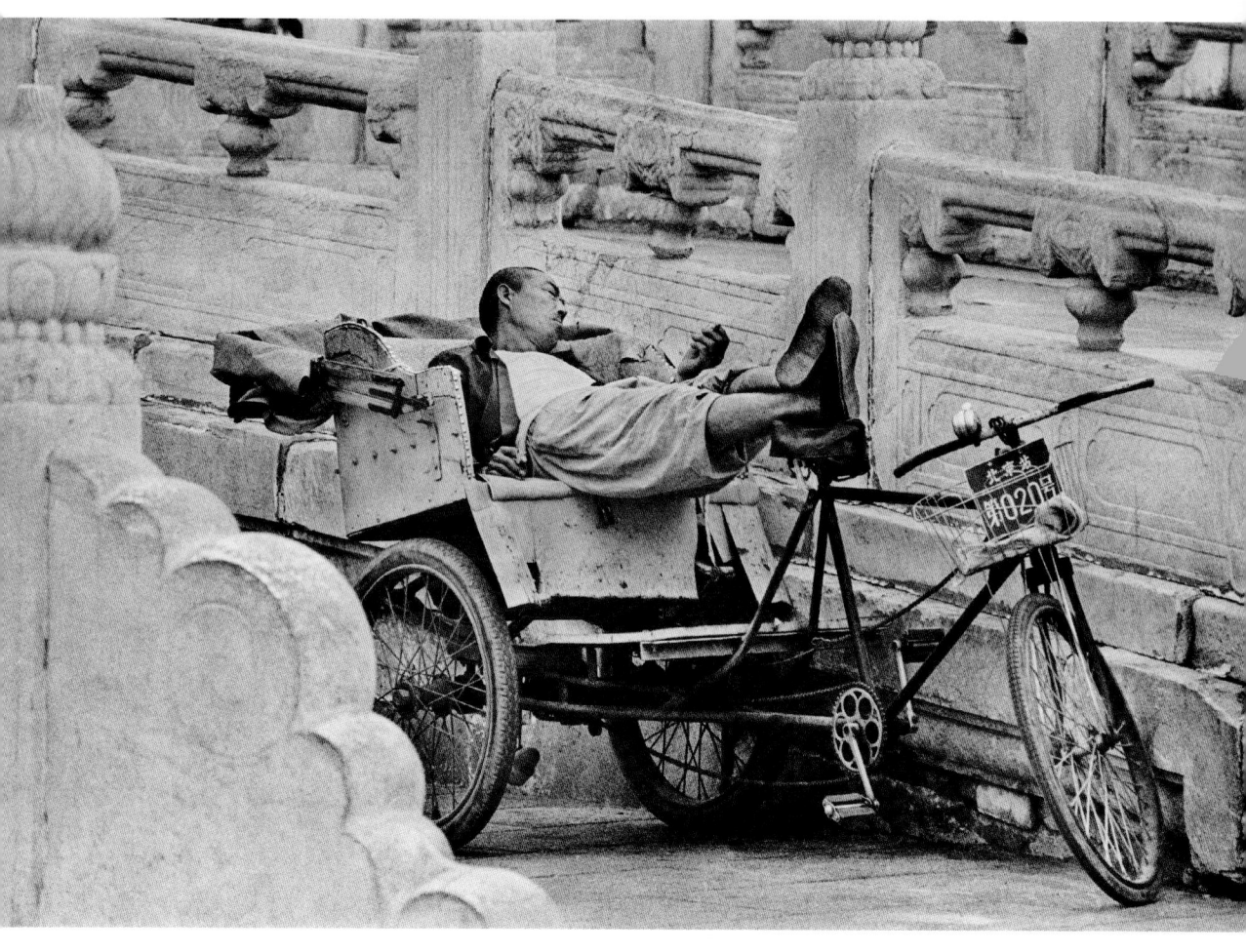

1984.5

京城无处不歇脚
Resting on a rickshaw

北京天安门金水桥
Golden Water Bridge, Tian'anmen, Beijing

2007.6

北京前门

Qianmen, Beijing

前门楼子梦中游

Resting on roadside

1984.4

提笼架鸟广场行

Taking a walk with pet birds

北京天安门广场

Tian'anmen Square, Beijing

1990.10

北京故宫
Palace Museum, Beijing

笼里笼外啥滋味
Caged birds on the tree

1986.10

各家鸟啼大比拼
A singing competition for pet birds

北京前门
Qianmen, Beijing

2005.10

北京玉渊潭
Yuyuantan Park, Beijing

保驾护航"九头鸟"
Birds on a bicycle

1994.5

自行车的"门诊部"
A bicycle repair stall

辽宁营口
Yingkou, Liaoning

2016.12

北京海淀
Haidian District, Beijing

手里活计忙不完
A bicycle repairer busy in work

1982.3

城镇无处不乒乓
Playing table tennis on a self-made table

福建泉州
Quanzhou, Fujian

2008.8

北京双吉胡同
Shuangji Hutong, Beijing

奥运场外摆擂台
A table tennis match outside Olympics venues

1994·5

田间地头台球赛
Playing snookers near the croplands

山东蓬莱
Penglai, Shandong

2007.12

河北石家庄
Shijiazhuang, Hebei

个个争当丁俊晖
Everyone wants to become another Ding Junhui

有其父必有其子
A father and his son playing soccer

1981.11

北京朝阳门
Chaoyangmen, Beijing

2005.10

北京王府井 街头滑板大比拼
Wangfujing, Beijing A street skateboarding competition

找个地方就蹦迪
Disco dancing on the street

1980.4

北京海淀
Haidian District, Beijing

2018.8

浙江宁波
Ningbo, Zhejiang

亭台楼阁交谊舞
Dancing in the park

1990.4

场内场外掀高潮

河南嵩县

Climbing onto the trees to watch games

Songxian, Henan

2015.5

北京朝阳
Chaoyang District, Beijing

社区热练钢管舞
Practicing pole dance in a local community

1989.1

撑天伏地罗汉功

People of various ages doing physical exercises

北京地坛

Temple of Earth, Beijing

2014.12

北京王府井
Wangfujing, Beijing

霹雳摇滚街头舞
Dancing on the street

1982

舞动太极真功夫
Practicing taichi

上海外滩
The Bund, Shanghai

2004.9

四川成都
Chengdu, Sichuan

你来我往巧过招
Practicing taichi in couples

1983.6

一日之计在于晨
Doing exercises before going to work

北京天安门广场
Tian'anmen Square, Beijing

2008.8

北京大学
Peking University, Beijing

燕园绿地太极阵
Figurines practicing taichi in Yanyuan Garden

1985.12

百炼成钢边防线
Soldiers in training

云南老山
Laoshan, Yunnan

2014.5

江苏镇江
Zhenjiang, Jiangsu

各得其乐练习课
The elderly and the young having their own fun

1985.4

万人国际马拉松
An international marathon

北京东二环
East Second Ring Road, Beijing

2008.8

北京国家体育场　　　　　　　　　　　　　　　　　　　　　　　　奥运开幕聚鸟巢

National Stadium, Beijing　　　　　　　　　　A crowd celebrating the opening of the Beijing Olympics

1997.4

成双成对乐自来　　　　　　　　　　　　　陕西西安
Lovers in pairs　　　　　　　　　　　　　Xi'an, Shaanxi

2014.12

海南三亚
Sanya, Hainan

面对面与背对背
Face-to-face and back-to-back

2004.10

东南西北中发白 浙江宁波
Playing mahjong Ningbo, Zhejiang

2014.12

北京朝阳
Chaoyang District, Beijing

时尚装饰麻将牌
A wall decorated with mahjong

1990.8

楚河汉界逐对杀
Playing Chinese chess

宁夏吴忠
Wuzhong, Ningxia

2017.8

北京钟鼓楼

Zhonggulou, Beijing

棋逢对手此时无

A kid playing Chinese chess alone

说学逗唱甩包袱
A cross talk performance

1986.2

北京地坛
Temple of Earth, Beijing

2018.2

河南宝丰　　　　　　　　　　　　　　　　　　　　马街书会二人转

Baofeng, Henan　　　　A song-and-dance duet performance at the Majie Folk Art Fair

笛箫锣鼓奏古乐
Playing ancient music with traditional instruments

1987.9

河北固安
Gu'an, Hebei

2018.2

河南宝丰
Baofeng, Henan

民间说唱摆龙门
A folk storytelling performance

1999.8

真真假假梦里寻
A kid sleeping amidst a pile of antiques

北京潘家园
Panjiayuan, Beijing

2014.1

北京潘家园

Panjiayuan, Beijing

琳琅满目任你挑

An antique stall

1982.3

城市卫生宣传日

A parade celebrating the Urban Cleaning Day

浙江杭州

Hangzhou, Zhejiang

2015.2

四川富顺
Fushun, Sichuan

扫除一切害人虫
A store selling pesticides

1981.7

电视进入百姓家
Buying television sets

北京西单商场
Xidan Department Store, Beijing

2017.8

北京山姆会员店
Sam's Club, Beijing

目不转睛液晶屏
A kid watching LCD televisions in a supermarket

1987.6

进口指标提大件

Quota certificates were needed to buy imported home appliances in the past

北京东城

Dongcheng District, Beijing

2014.3

云南元阳
Yuanyang, Yunnan

电器多大都能扛
Carrying a newly bought refrigerator home

1989.1

大庭广众看直播
Watching "live broadcast" on the street

上海老城
Old District of Shanghai

2005.10

北京王府井大街

Wangfujing Street, Beijing

一个人的大屏幕

A big screen for one person

雨后春笋民营起

Private enterprises flourishing after reform and opening up

1987.3

广东深圳

Shenzhen, Guangdong

2005.6

江苏苏州
Suzhou, Jiangsu

外企入驻产业园
A foreign-funded company in the industrial development zone

风雪签证大使馆

People lining up to apply for visa outside the embassy in Beijing despite heavy snow

1990.1

北京秀水街

Xiushui Street, Beijing

2012.10

北京出入境管理大厅
Beijing Visa Center, Beijing

北京迎纳八方客
Welcome to Beijing

如此命名太荒诞

A visitor in front of a painting for fortune telling

1989.1

北京中国美术馆

National Art Museum of China, Beijing

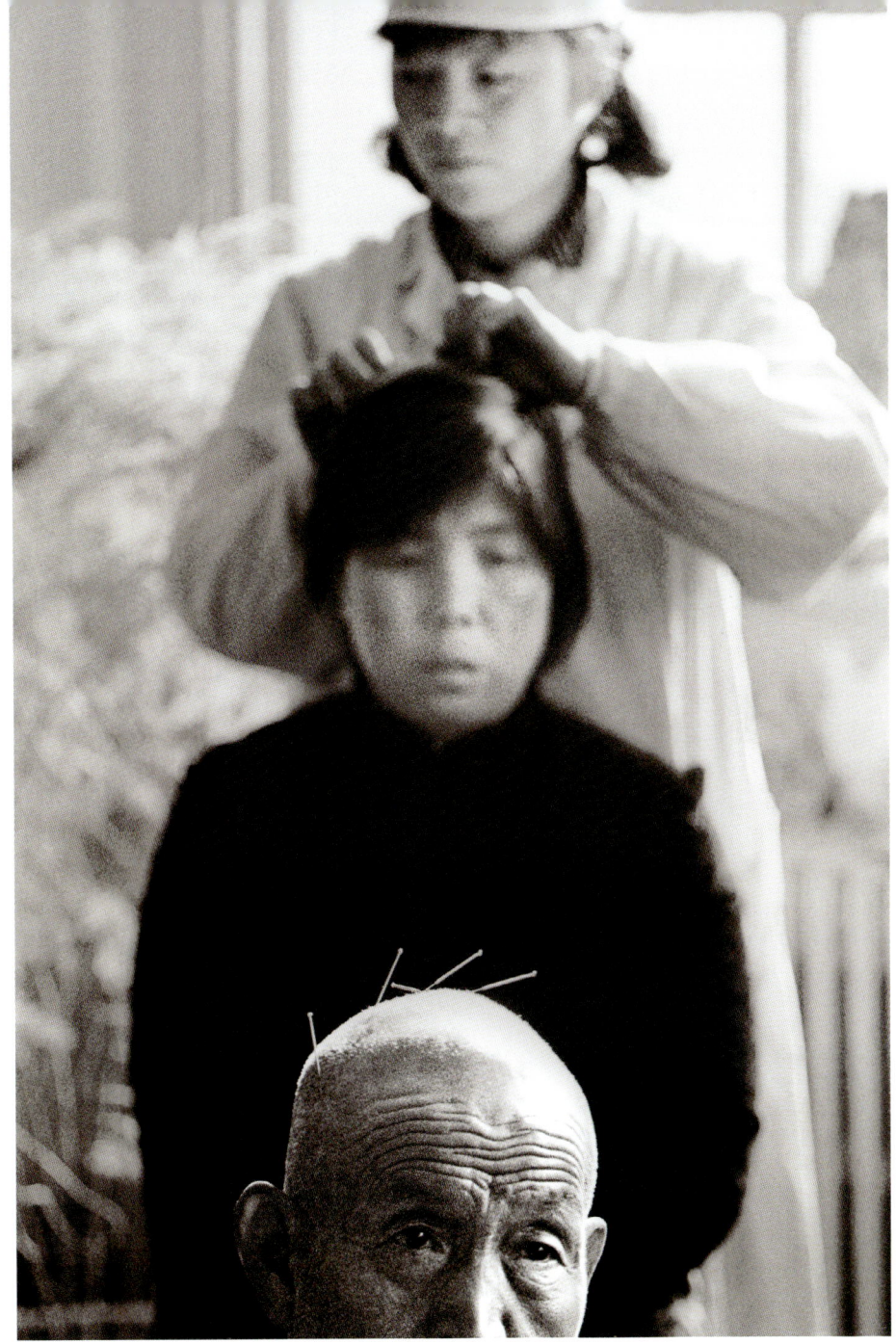

1992.2

山西运城
Yuncheng, Shanxi

头顶银针通经络
Taking an acupuncture therapy

2005.9

大病小病齐吊瓶
Taking transfusions in hospital

山东济南
Jinan, Shandong

2013.11

湖南凤凰
Fenghuang, Hunan

点滴想把百病除
Patients taking transfusions at a clinic

1996.1

传呼信息电话回

Answering a messenger call via paid phone

北京羊肉胡同

Yangrou Hutong, Beijing

2005.10

北京王府井大街

Wangfujing Street, Beijing

移动联通信天游

A huge model of a mobile phone

2012.10

遍地开花福彩摊
At a welfare lottery station

北京石景山
Shijingshan District, Beijing

2018.8

浙江宁波
Ningbo, Zhejiang

从牛到熊都喂过
At a stock exchange center

1983.1

全民普法宣传日
An event promoting public legal literacy

北京东城
Dongcheng District, Beijing

2018.3

河南宝丰

Baofeng, Henan

反腐倡廉学包公

An event promoting honest government

1983.10

日夜奋战葛洲坝
Constructors of Gezhouba Hydropower Station

湖北宜昌
Yichang, Hubei

2007.10

北京朝阳

Chaoyang District, Beijing

盘古鸟巢水立方

Constructors of Pangu Plaza, with the Bird's Nest and the Water Cube in the background

重修长城筑国魂

Rebuilding the Great Wall to promote national spirit

1984.9

北京八达岭

Badaling, Beijing

2013.9

陕西延川
Yanchuan, Shaanxi

黄河岸边微景观
A miniature "Great Wall" on the bank of the Yellow River

1987.12

钢铁长城筑南疆
A steel Great Wall defending the southern border

云南老山
Laoshan, Yunnan

2014.10

北京天安门广场 广场漫步隔代人
Tian'anmen Square, Beijing An elderly veteran and his grandson at Tian'anmen Square

观澜

一位摄影记者眼中的改革开放

Lan's Lens
— China's Reform & Opening Up
in the Eyes of a Photojournalist

1991.7

两个轮子的王国
A kingdom of bicycles

上海光新路
Guangxin Road, Shanghai

2005.12

北京北四环
North Fourth Ring Road, Beijing

四个轱辘遍京城
A Beijing road crowded with vehicles during rush hours

1981.4

长安街头无轿车
A kingdom of bicycles

北京西长安街
West Chang'an Avenue, Beijing

2012.4

北京东长安街

East Chang'an Avenue, Beijing

车水马龙贯东西

A country on the wheels

1981.5

四方交通我指挥
A traffic police officer

北京东长安街
East Chang'an Avenue, Beijing

2008.9

北京交通管理局指挥大厅
Commanding Center of Beijing Traffic Management Bureau, Beijing

运行中枢大本营
The command for urban traffic management

这种时候我也有
A bicycler violating traffic rules attracting a crowd of onlookers

1979·7

北京东单
Dongdan, Beijing

2015.12

北京天安门广场 好在我没被拦过

Tian'anmen Square, Beijing Police officers stopping a car that violates traffic rules

排队打的出行难
Waiting for cabs

1984.12

北京饭店
Beijing Hotel, Beijing

2008.11

北京前门大街

Qianmen Street, Beijing

即叫即停送客忙

Taxis on the street

当时没改步行街

A bus stop at Wangfujing before it was transformed into a pedestrian street

1982.4

北京王府井

Wangfujing, Beijing

2018.9

北京煤市街

Meishi Street, Beijing

公共交通是首选

Waiting for a bus

1985.10

乡村客运超负荷

A bus overloaded with passengers in rural China

贵州锦屏

Jinping, Guizhou

2008.8

北京前门

Qianmen, Beijing

公交运营路路通

A tour bus bearing advertisement of Lenovo

1995.11

城区骑士齐出巡
Patrol men on horsebacks

山西太原
Taiyuan, Shanxi

2008.8

北京朝阳

Chaoyang District, Beijing

安全驾驶守护神

Protectors of safe transport

1998.8

十次事故九次快

A traffic accident

北京海淀

Haidian District, Beijing

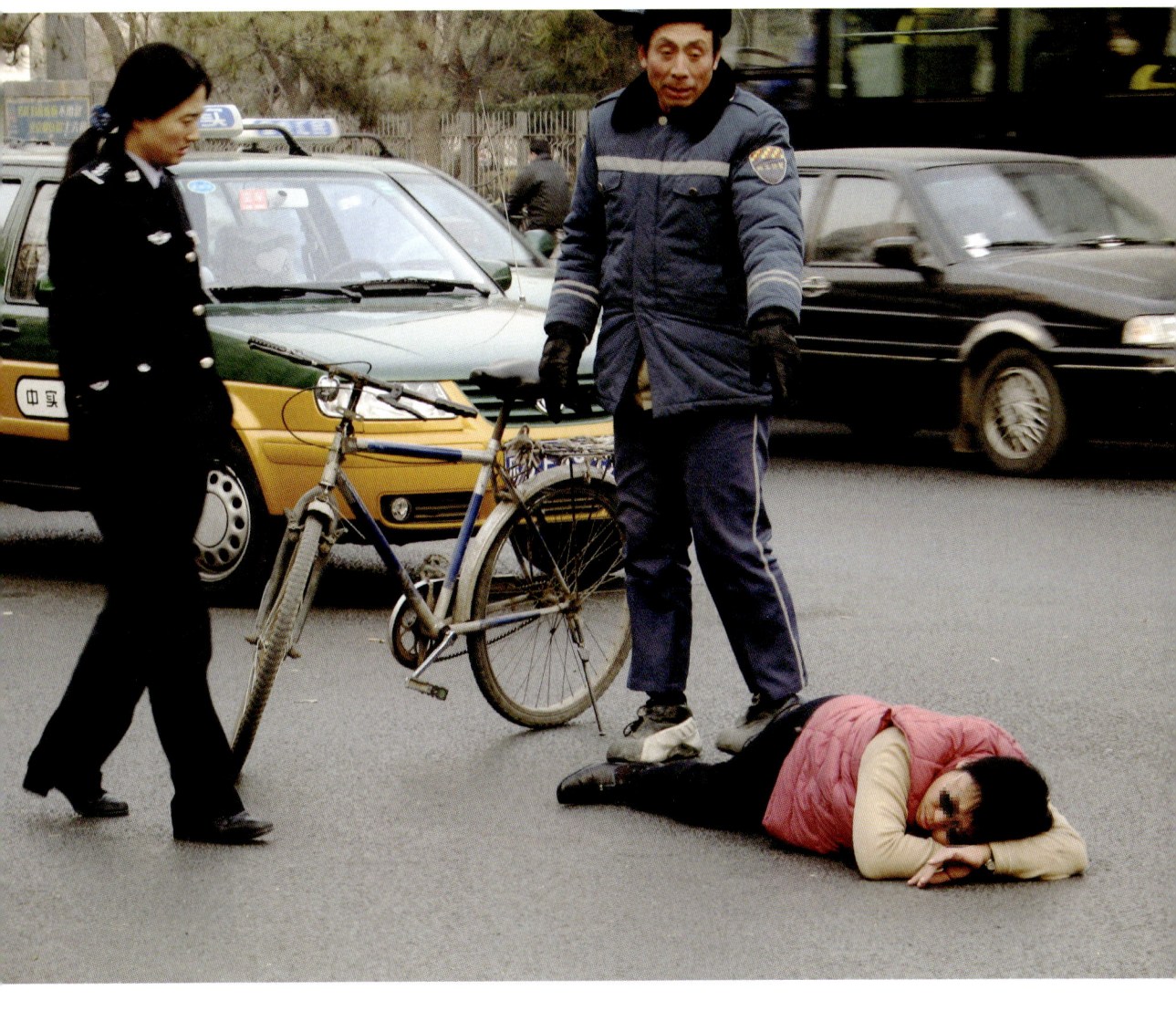

2005.12

北京朝阳

Chaoyang District, Beijing

交通协管遇难题

A traffic accident involving a traffic police assistant

没有过不去的坎
A man riding a bicycle passing through roadblocks

2004.9

山西平遥
Pingyao, Shanxi

2015.6

北京西城
Xicheng District, Beijing

道路拥堵奈我何
A man riding a bicycle in a stream of cars

2000.4

我是一条变色龙
A man riding a round-shape cycle

北京木樨地
Muxidi, Beijing

2003.8

上海浦东   上下踩踏风火轮

Pudong, Shanghai   BMX cycling

1987.11

高峰犹如赶大集

Rush hours

广东广州

Guangzhou, Guangdong

2017.6

北京朝阳
Chaoyang District, Beijing

共享单车调配急
Shared bicycles

1988.7

哪一个都不能少
Kids in trolleys

北京府学胡同
Fuxue Hutong, Beijing

2014.4

北京顺义
Shunyi District, Beijing

这里诞生赛车手
Future racing drivers

1993.5

看看谁能跑过谁
Which is faster?

江苏无锡
Wuxi, Jiangsu

2012.4

江苏徐州
Xuzhou, Jiangsu

谁的座驾都敢挡
A little bicycler racing with a horse

车马步行碰头会

Car, bicycle, horse-dragging cart and pedestrian

1985.4

北京怀柔

Huairou District, Beijing

2010.4

北京石景山
Shijingshan District, Beijing

前方修路规矩多
A traffic sign at the entrance to a road under renovation

1988.4

没有过不去的河
A ferry crossing the river

广西龙胜
Longsheng, Guangxi

2012.8

陕西府谷
Fugu, Shaanxi

黄河古渡运输忙
A ferry transporting passengers across the Yellow River

1981.7

红灯停后绿灯行
Waiting for the green light at an intersection

北京东单
Dongdan, Beijing

2016.6

北京前门

Qianmen, Beijing

古都胡同带您游

A rickshaw driver waiting for tourists in Beijing

1996.5

旧品回收一家人
A garbage recycler and his family

北京北新桥
Beixinqiao, Beijing

2013.7

北京昌平 饮料废罐筑成墙
Changping District, Beijing A wall laid by recycled garbage

2009.2

农民研制机器人
A robot invented by a local farmer

北京通州
Tongzhou District, Beijing

2014.4

江苏南京
Nanjing, Jiangsu

秦淮河畔任你游
Riding a rickshaw for a night tour along the Qinhuai River

1989.3

同车共济不怕难

河北固安

Fearing no long, tough journey

Gu'an, Hebei

1991.7

浙江温州
Wenzhou, Zhejiang

满载负荷轻松走
An overloaded cart

铺天盖地还敢开

A walking tractor overloaded with straw

1990.8

宁夏吴忠

Wuzhong, Ningxia

2012.10

北京门头沟

Mentougou District, Beijing

加足马力把路赶

A cart overloaded with recycled garbage

拖拉满载赶海人
A tractor overloaded with passengers

1994.5

山东威海
Weihai, Shandong

2014.7

北京海淀
Haidian District, Beijing

上下夜班护路工
Road maintainers after a night's work

1981.7

蒸汽年代成往事
Steam locomotive in the past

北京永定门火车站
Yongdingmen Railway Station, Beijing

2007.12

北京西站
Beijing West Railway Station, Beijing

和谐之旅高速行
A CRH bullet train berthing at the station

1992.4

京城打工第一站
The first station for migrant workers in Beijing

北京雍和宫
Yonghegong, Beijing

2009.10

陕西西安
Xi'an, Shaanxi

水电木工我都行
Migrant workers waiting for employers

1985.5

左西右东如何走
Confusing road guide

北京景山
Jingshan Park, Beijing

1996.4

上海静安
Jing'an District, Shanghai

指东道西你来猜
Asking for the way

2001.3

小天使与白天鹅
Little "angels" and a white swan

北京动物园
Beijing Zoo, Beijing

2008.8

北京北翔凤胡同
Beixiangfeng Hutong, Beijing

遛猫遛狗遛鸭子
Walking the duck

2007.7

疑似哪吒天外来
Little roller skaters in rest

江苏徐州
Xuzhou, Jiangsu

2017.8

湖南长沙
Changsha, Hunan

星空变幻遇梵高
Sitting in Van Gogh's *Starry Night*

我的宝贝在哪里
Parents picking their kids after school

1987.5

北京三里屯
Sanlitun, Beijing

2017.10

山西怀仁

Huairen, Shanxi

您是来接我的吧

A pupil meeting his parents after school

以身作则安全行

Abiding by traffic rules by walking along the crosswalk

1982.3

上海外滩

The Bund, Shanghai

2018.9

上海外滩
The Bund, Shanghai

放心之旅一线牵
A mother linked with her kid with a rope

1994.7

前仆后继幸福来

Today's happy life credited to sacrifice of our forefathers

上海黄浦公园

Huangpu Park, Shanghai

1991.7

上海黄浦
Huangpu, Shanghai

画里画外恋人行
Two couples of lovers

1989.7

闺蜜防晒一个盆　　　　　　　　　　　　　　　　北京金台路

A couple of besties　　　　　　　　　　　　　Jintai Road, Beijing

1995.8

北京展览馆
Beijing Exhibition Center, Beijing

骤雨暴风一把伞
Sharing the same umbrella in heavy rain

1982.4

春天烦恼何时休
A windy day in spring

北京前门
Qianmen, Beijing

2006.4

北京门头沟
Mentougou District, Beijing

北风吹来沙与尘
North wind bringing sand

1982.2

从千军台到庄户
Folk art tour from Qianjuntai to Zhuanghu Village

北京门头沟
Mentougou District, Beijing

2015.3

北京门头沟
Mentougou District, Beijing

正月十五古幡会
The Ancient Flag Fair in celebration of the Lantern Festival

1986.8

门庭若市紫禁城

The Palace Museum crowded with tourists

北京故宫

Palace Museum, Beijing

2016.5

江苏周庄
Zhouzhuang, Jiangsu

川流不息古镇游
Zhouzhuang Town crowded with tourists

广场是我大课堂
A "class" at Tian'anmen Square

1984·7

北京天安门广场
Tian'anmen Square, Beijing

2017.8

北京天安门广场

Tian'anmen Square, Beijing

北京城中觅佳境

A tourist consulting a map

1993.3

代表委员聚一堂

NPC and CPPCC under the same roof

北京人民大会堂

Great Hall of the People, Beijing

2013.3

北京人民大会堂 方针政策传四方
Great Hall of the People, Beijing Attendees leaving the venue after the meeting

两会热点扎成堆

A crowd of journalists interviewing a delegate during the Two Sessions

1993·3

北京人民大会堂

Great Hall of the People, Beijing

2015.8

北京天安门广场

Tian'anmen Square, Beijing

现场新闻自媒体

Journalists taking photos with their mobile phones

钢铁长城振国威
A military parade

1984.10

北京天安门广场
Tian'anmen Square, Beijing

2015.9

北京天安门广场
Tian'anmen Square, Beijing

好汉方显当年勇
Veterans during a military parade

1999.10

全球直播遍五洲
Journalists from around the world reporting China's Two Sessions

北京天安门广场
Tian'anmen Square, Beijing

2009.10

北京天安门广场
Tian'anmen Square, Beijing

举世瞩目传四海
China's Two Sessions attracting global attention

王文澜，中国日报社高级顾问，中国摄影家协会顾问。

参加过唐山大地震、老山前线、抗洪救灾等重大事件采访和党代会、全国人大、全国政协、各国首脑访华等重要时政新闻报道。

先后在全国新闻摄影优秀作品评选中荣获金、银、铜牌奖，并获得过中国新闻奖、中国新闻摄影学术贡献奖。荣获全国十佳摄影记者、全国十佳体育摄影记者、全国人像摄影十杰等称号。先后担任全国影展、国际影展、新闻影展、中国摄影金像奖和国家图书奖评委。

已策划、编辑、出版《京味》《名人透视》《流动的长城》《瞬间》《中国纪事》《自行车的日子》《偶然》《地平线》《家国细节》《动感亚洲》《时代肖像》以及"百名摄影师聚焦"系列画册。

曾在中国美术馆举办《广场漫步》和《中外新闻人像》摄影展，在中国社会科学院新闻研究所、北京大学、中国新闻学院、北京电影学院、人民日报、新华社等单位讲授新闻摄影。

Wang Wenlan is a senior advisor to *China Daily* and an advisor to China Photographers Association.

He worked as a photojournalist to report such breaking news stories as the Tangshan Earthquake, China's self-defense counterattack against Vietnam at Laoshan, and flood relief campaigns, as well as such important events as the National Congress of the Communist Party of China (CPC), the annual sessions of the National People's Congress (NPC) and the National Committee of the Chinese People's Political Consultative Conference (CPPCC), and foreign heads of state's visits to China.

His photographic works have received gold, silver and bronze prizes at many national photojournalism contests and the China News Award, as well as the China Award of Academic Contribution for Photojournalism. In addition, he has won many titles and prizes such as one of China's Top 10 Photojournalists, Top 10 Sports Photojournalists and Top 10 Portrait Photographers. He has consecutively served as a jury member for national and international photography exhibitions, news photography exhibitions, the Golden Statue Awards for Chinese Photography, and the China National Book Awards.

He has planned, compiled and published books including *Flavor of Beijing*, *Insight into Celebrities*, *The Flowing Great Wall*, *Moments*, *Documenting China*, *The Life of Bicycles in China*, *Once Upon a Time in China*, *Horizon*, *Trifles of Family and Nation*, *Dynamic Asia*, *Portraits of Our Times*, and a dozen volumes of the photo book series "Focus of 100 Photographers."

He ever held solo photography exhibitions "Roaming around the Square" and "Chinese and Foreign News Portraits" at the National Art Museum of China, and gave lectures on photojournalism at universities and media organizations such as the Institute of Journalism and Communications Studies under the Chinese Academy of Social Sciences, Peking University, China Journalism College, Beijing Film Academy, *People's Daily*, and Xinhua News Agency.